THE
Human Head

by Kathy Allen

Consultant:
Marjorie J. Hogan, MD
Associate Professor
University of Minnesota, Minneapolis

Capstone press

Mankato, Minnesota

Fact Finders is published by Capstone Press,
151 Good Counsel Drive, P.O. Box 669, Mankato, Minnesota 56002.
www.capstonepress.com

Library of Congress Cataloging-in-Publication Data
Allen, Kathy.
    The human head / by Kathy Allen.
    p. cm. — (Fact finders. Anatomy class)
    Includes bibliographical references and index.
    Summary: "Describes the anatomy of the human head, including organs, muscles, and the
skull" — Provided by publisher.
    ISBN 978-1-4296-3338-3 (library binding)
    ISBN 978-1-4296-3882-1 (softcover)
    1. Head — Juvenile literature. I. Title. II. Series.
QM535.A45 2010
611'.91 — dc22   2009002793

Editorial Credits
Lori Shores, editor; Ted Williams, designer; Svetlana Zhurkin, media researcher

Photo Credits
AP Images/Courtesy of Harvard Medical School, 21 (inset); Michael Dwyer, 21
Getty Images/3D4Medical, 17, 19, 29; AFP/Gabriel Bouys, 15
iStockphoto/Melissa King, 11
Photo Researchers, Inc./Anatomical Travelogue, 7; Prof Cinti & V. Gremet, 11 (inset)
Shutterstock/Aleksandr S. Khachunts, 9; Anastasios Kandris, 7 (inset); Anatomical Design, 23; Elena
    Elisseeva, 5; Larry St. Pierre, 27; Neo Edmund, 29 (inset); Scott Rothstein, 17 (inset); Sebastian
    Kaulitzki, 24;Vladimir Yessikov, 8
Svetlana Zhurkin, 12
Wikimedia/Patrick J. Lynch, medical illustrtator & C. Carl Jaffe, M.D., cardiologist, cover

Essential content terms are **bold** and are defined at the bottom of the page where they first appear.

Table of Contents

The Human Head

Look at your head in a mirror. What's the first thing you see? Maybe it's your eyes, nose, or skin. You might think of these features as separate parts. In fact, each part of the human head works together. Anatomy, the study of the human body, looks at body systems and their parts. The mouth is part of the respiratory system because it helps you breathe. It's also part of the digestive system because it helps you eat.

All of these systems are controlled by one amazing organ in your head. The brain is like mission control for your whole body. It controls the work that all the other parts do. In the human head, many systems and parts work together to make you a living person.

CHAPTER 1

On the Surface

You've probably looked at yourself in the mirror a million times. But take a closer look. Have you ever noticed all the cool things on the surface of your head? From your hair to your **pores**, the first layer of the human head is a sight to behold.

Skin: Magic Material

Imagine a material that is flexible and strong. If it tears, it repairs itself. It's waterproof, and it controls temperature. This material is your skin, and it's busy. Skin protects you from dirt and germs that could harm your body. The sweat from pores on your skin helps your body keep cool and get rid of waste. And as skin works, it oozes wax and oils that protect your skin and keep it soft.

> **pore** — one of the tiny holes in your skin through which you sweat

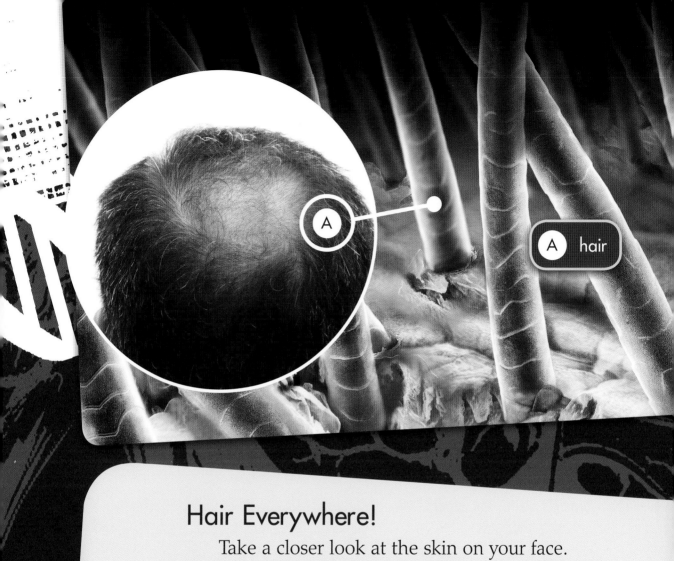

A — hair

Hair Everywhere!

Take a closer look at the skin on your face. Can you find a spot that isn't covered in hair? Your cheeks? Guess again. Fine hair covers most of your skin, even your cheeks. Skin is pierced by thousands of tubes called hair follicles. Your scalp alone has about 100,000 hair follicles. Curly, straight, brown, blonde — hair tells the world something about you. But that's not all it does. Hair also keeps you warm and protects your body.

Eyes and the Travel of Light

From the mass of skin and hair that is your head, your eyes look out to the world. When you look at something, what you actually see is light bouncing off an object. Your eyes turn light rays into images your brain can understand.

Light travels an amazing journey through your eyes. First the eye focuses the light. Next your eye takes a picture, sort of like a camera. The eye then sends information about the picture to your brain.

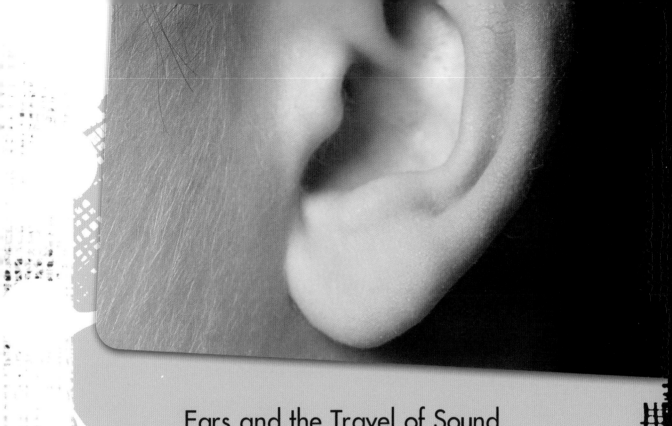

Ears and the Travel of Sound

Like your eyes, your ears are part of an amazing journey — the travel of sound. Sound waves are collected by your ear and sent through the ear canal. In the middle ear, sound waves vibrate the **eardrum**. The vibration moves three little bones. These bones send the vibrations to the inner ear. Tiny hairlike structures called cilia (SIH-lee-uh) send the vibrations as messages to the brain.

> **eardrum** — a thin piece of skin stretched tight like a drum inside the ear

The Mouth: A Multitasker

For a look inside the human head, all you have to do is open your mouth. You'll see some large parts, such as your tongue and teeth. But it's the smaller parts you can't see that make the mouth's work possible. **Saliva** pours into your mouth from **glands** below the back teeth and under the tongue. Saliva makes it easier to chew food and to speak. Just think of how hard it is to talk when your mouth is dry!

saliva — the clear liquid in your mouth that helps you swallow and begin to digest food

gland — an organ that either produces chemicals or allows substances to leave the body

BODY FACT

Like your skin, the membrane on the inside of your mouth is strong. It can stand a lot of wear and tear, like when you bite your lip.

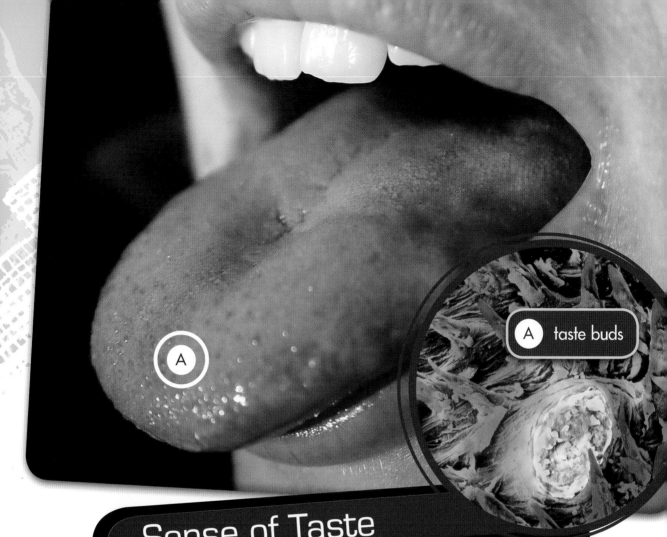

A

A taste buds

Sense of Taste

Hidden in the little bumps on your tongue are about 10,000 taste buds. These tiny organs respond to tastes such as sweet, salty, sour, and bitter. Taste buds send messages to the brain about how something tastes. But taste buds only respond to liquid. Dry food in a mouth with no saliva would have no taste at all.

The Nose: A Gatekeeper

You can also look inside your nose. But deep inside your nose there are thousands of cells you can't see. These cells react to chemicals coming off your gym socks and other smelly objects. The cells send messages to your brain about the way the socks smell.

But 95 percent of the nose plays no role in smelling. Your nose's biggest job is to filter the air you breathe. The nose traps dust and bacteria in slimy **mucus**. You swallow the mucus to keep the dust and bacteria away from your lungs.

mucus — a sticky liquid that coats the inside of the nose, throat, and mouth

BODY FACT

The average person can recognize about 10,000 different smells.

CHAPTER 2

The Next Layer

Just beneath your skin, there are a bunch of parts you couldn't do without. Smiling and talking would be impossible without them. Thanks to your muscles and bones, your head can lead the way.

The Constant Work of Muscle

The human face is a bundle of movement, from blinking and winking to speaking and chewing. If you could see through your skin, you would see the muscles that make this movement possible. Muscles can only pull a bone. They can't push. Muscles work in pairs so you can move a body part in more than one direction.

Movement in your face happens more often than you might think. Your eye muscles move about 100,000 times a day. Your face alone has more than 30 muscles. Sometimes you move these muscles on purpose, such as when you make a funny face. But other movements, like blinking, you don't even think about.

BODY FACT

The average person blinks
15 times each minute.

Bones: Living Armor

The 29 bones of your skull give your head a shape and protect what's inside. Flat bones protect your brain. These bones are connected like the pieces of a jigsaw puzzle. The 14 bones of the face are shaped to protect different parts of the head, such as your eyes and nose. These bones are stronger than concrete, yet light enough so you can still lift your head.

While the skull is like armor for your head, it is also alive and constantly working. Bones are living organs. Each bone creates blood cells in its soft, spongy center, called the **marrow**.

marrow — the soft substance inside bones where blood cells are made

BODY FACT

The only bone of the skull that can move is the jawbone.

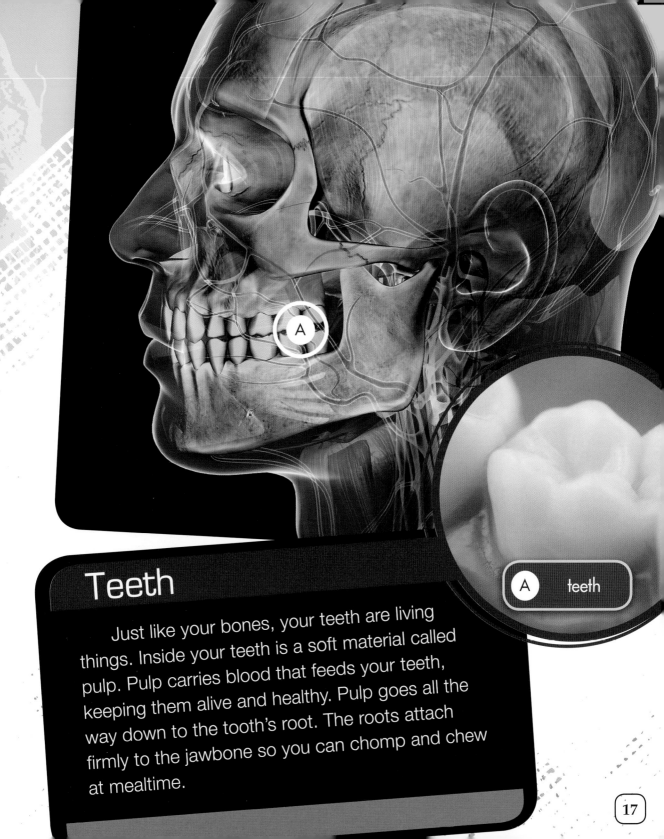

Teeth

Just like your bones, your teeth are living things. Inside your teeth is a soft material called pulp. Pulp carries blood that feeds your teeth, keeping them alive and healthy. Pulp goes all the way down to the tooth's root. The roots attach firmly to the jawbone so you can chomp and chew at mealtime.

A   teeth

Blood: Food for Your Head

A network of blood vessels runs all over in the muscles and bones of your head. Through these tubes, the heart pumps oxygen-rich blood to every part of your head. Muscles and organs, such as your brain, need this oxygen to live.

The carotid **arteries** supply blood to your head. Put your fingers on either side of your neck just below your chin. You can feel these arteries pulse as blood flows through them.

artery — a large blood vessel that carries blood away from the heart

BODY FACT

Strung together, all the blood vessels in your body could circle the earth two and a half times.

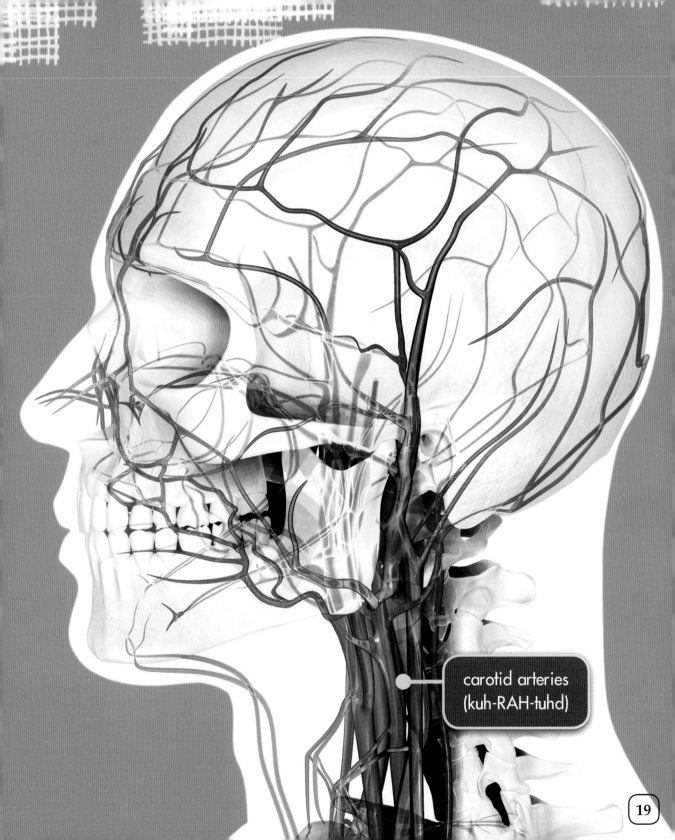

carotid arteries
(kuh-RAH-tuhd)

CHAPTER 3

The Brain: Mission Control

The parts of your head would be of little use without one big organ called the brain. The brain is part of the nervous system. This system allows you to interact with the world. The nervous system also includes the **spinal cord** and a network of **nerves** throughout your body. Nerves in your hand tell your brain when you touch a hot burner. Your brain answers by pulling your hand away from the heat. Your nervous system also controls breathing and other movements you do without thinking.

> **spinal cord** — a thick cord of nerve tissue in the neck and back
> **nerve** — a thin fiber that sends messages between your brain and other parts of your body

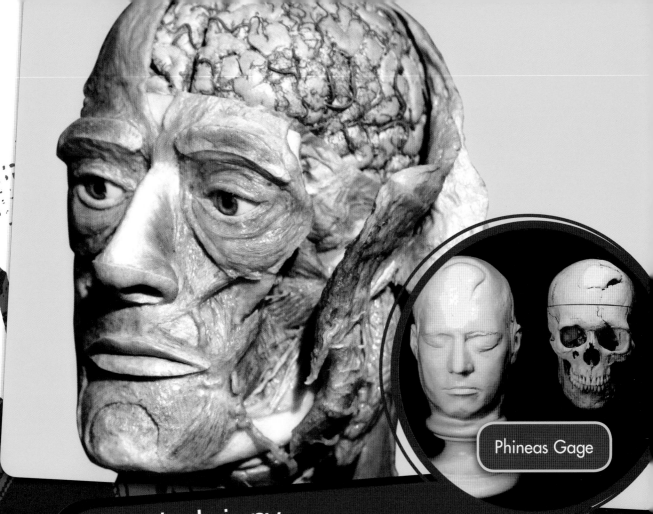

Phineas Gage

Brain Injury

Much of what we know about the brain comes from studying brain injuries. The most famous case of brain injury happened to the unlucky Phineas Gage. In 1848, an explosion sent an iron rod more than 3 feet (.9 meter) long through Gage's head. The injury destroyed the left side of his brain. Amazingly, Gage survived, but friends said he became rude and unpredictable. Scientists learned from Gage that injuries to specific parts of the brain affect personality and behavior.

Bumpy, Lumpy Brain Parts

The machine that is your brain is made of several parts. The biggest part is the cerebrum (suh-REE-brum). The cerebrum is divided into four sections called lobes. Each lobe has an important job. When you make a decision or feel an emotion, that's the work of the frontal lobe. The parietal lobe understands information such as taste and temperature. Memory and learning take place in the temporal lobe. And the occipital lobe helps you understand what you see.

The second-largest part of your brain is called the cerebellum. This part is near the back and bottom of your brain. When you use your eyes, legs, and arms to catch a football, you can thank your cerebellum. It coordinates your body's movement and balance.

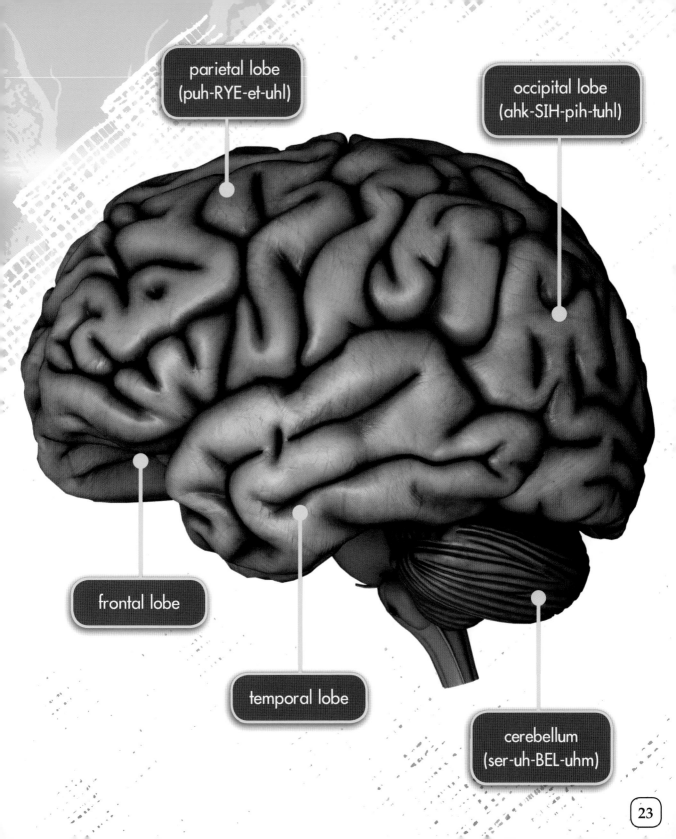

parietal lobe
(puh-RYE-et-uhl)

occipital lobe
(ahk-SIH-pih-tuhl)

frontal lobe

temporal lobe

cerebellum
(ser-uh-BEL-uhm)

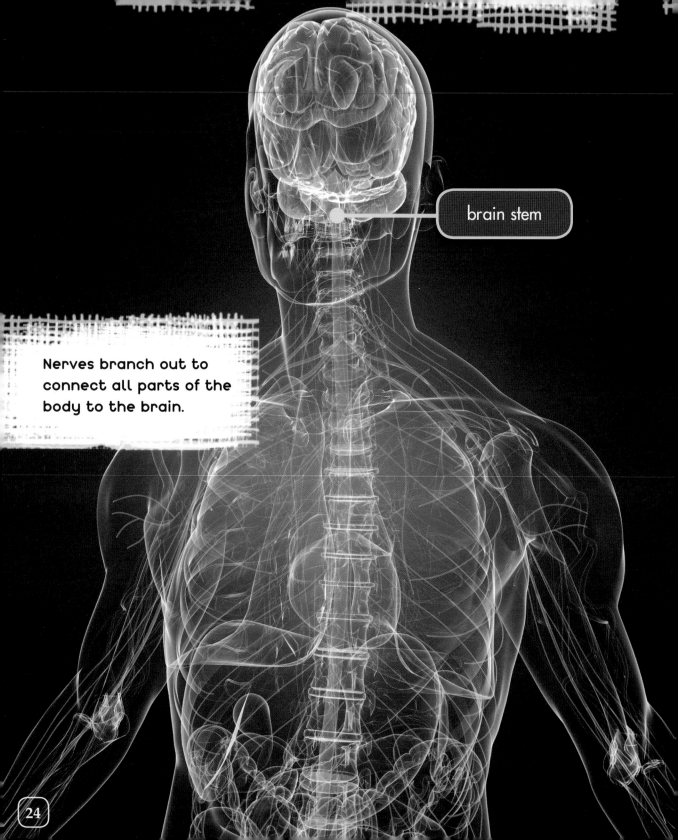

brain stem

Nerves branch out to connect all parts of the body to the brain.

The Brain Stem

Messages between your brain and body travel through the brain stem. This bundle of nerves is located at the base of the brain. The brain stem connects the brain to the spinal cord. The spinal cord helps deliver the brain's messages to all parts of the body.

But the brain stem is more than a message center. It controls the activities you need to stay alive, including your heart rate and breathing. The brain stem also controls when you sleep and how alert you are when you're awake.

Thanks to Your Brain

Your body is constantly moving. You run with your legs and speak with your mouth. But it's your brain that makes you a living person. For example, your eyes do a lot of work to focus light. But it's the brain that actually sees. Think about when you race your friend on the playground. It's your brain that tells your legs to move.

CHAPTER 4

Always Working

The human head is in a constant state of activity. This activity includes the travel of sound through the ears, blood through the arteries, and messages through the nervous system. The brain understands each message from the sense organs and responds as needed.

Even while you're reading this book, the muscles of your face are contracted. Your eyes focus the light that allows you to see the words. Your ears receive sounds all around you. Meanwhile, your salivary glands are busy responding to the smell of lunch picked up by your nose. The human head is an amazing combination of the systems at work in the busy machine that is your body. You'd really be lost without your head!

Head Diagram

A   **Skin** — Skin is an organ, like your heart or brain. It is the largest organ of your body.

B   **Eyes** — Your eye lens sits just behind the iris, which is the colored part of the eye.

C   **Nose** — The tiny, stiff hairs in your nose help to keep dust and dirt out of your lungs.

D   **Mouth** — Every day, glands in your mouth make about 3 pints (1.4 liters) of saliva.

E   **Teeth** — Tooth enamel is strong, but acids from bacteria in your mouth can eat a hole right through your teeth.

F   **Brain** — The brain contains more than 10 billion nerve cells.

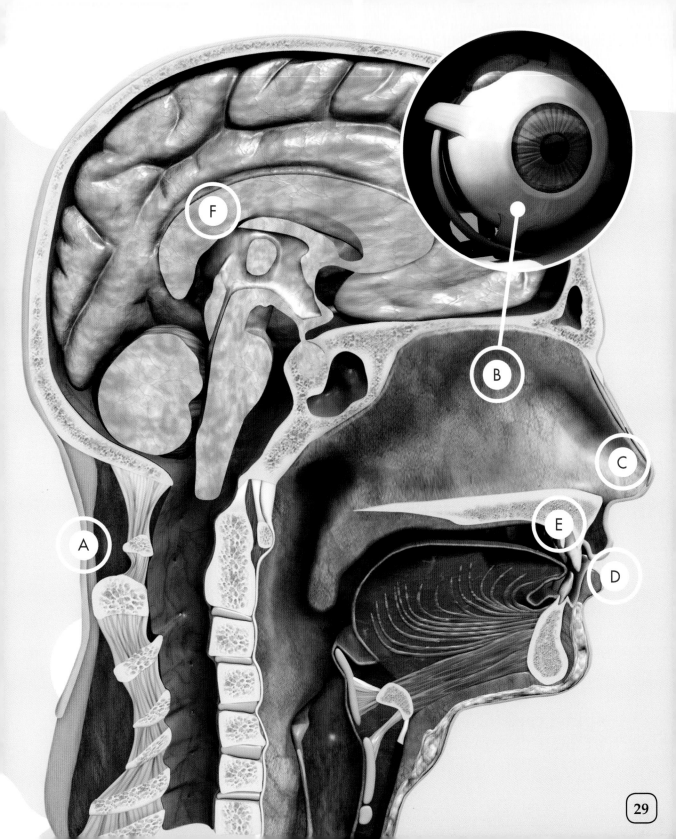

Glossary

artery (AR-tuh-ree) — a large blood vessel that carries blood away from the heart

eardrum (EER-druhm) — a thin piece of skin stretched tight like a drum inside the ear; the eardrum vibrates when sound waves strike it.

gland (GLAND) — an organ that either produces chemicals or allows substances to leave the body

marrow (MA-roh) — the soft substance inside bones where blood cells are made

mucus (MYOO-kuhss) — a sticky liquid that coats the inside of the nose, throat, and mouth

nerve (NURV) — a thin fiber that sends messages between your brain and other parts of your body

pore (POR) — one of the tiny holes in your skin through which you sweat

saliva (suh-LYE-vuh) — the clear liquid in your mouth that helps you swallow and begin to digest food

spinal cord (SPY-nuhl KORD) — a thick cord of nerve tissue in the neck and back; the spinal cord links the brain to the body's other nerves.

Read More

Burstein, John. *The Astounding Nervous System: How Does My Brain Work?* Slim Goodbody's Body Buddies. New York: Crabtree, 2009.

Macaulay, David. *The Way We Work: Getting to Know the Amazing Human Body.* Boston: Houghton Mifflin, 2008.

Smith, Miranda. *Human Body.* Navigators. New York: Kingfisher, 2008.

Internet Sites

FactHound offers a safe, fun way to find Internet sites related to this book. All of the sites on FactHound have been researched by our staff.

Here's all you do:

Visit *www.facthound.com*

FactHound will fetch the best sites for you!

Index